Rocks and Fossils

KINGFISHER

Kingfisher Publications Plc
New Penderel House,
283–288 High Holborn,
London WC1V 7HZ
www.kingfisherpub.com

Published in paperback by Kingfisher Publications 2006
First published in hardback by Kingfisher Publications Plc 2003
2 4 6 8 10 9 7 5 3 1
1TR/1005/PROSP/RNB(RNB)/140MA/F

Copyright © Kingfisher Publications Plc 2006

ISBN-13: 978 0 7534 0860 5
ISBN-10: 0 7534 0860 0

Senior editor: Carron Brown
Designers: Melissa Alaverdy, Paul Akins
Picture manager: Cee Weston-Baker
Picture researcher: Rachael Swann
DTP manager: Nicky Studdart
Artwork archivists: Wendy Allison, Jenny Lord
Senior production controller: Nancy Roberts
Indexer: Chris Bernstein

Printed in China

Acknowledgements
The publishers would like to thank the following for permission to reproduce their material. Every care has been taken
to trace copyright holders. However, if there have been unintentional omissions or failure to trace copyright holders,
we apologise and will, if informed, endeavour to make corrections in any future edition.
b = bottom, *c* = centre, *l* = left, *t* = top, *r* = right

pages: *cover* Corbis; 1 Corbis; 2–3 Corbis; 4–5 Geoscience Features; 6–7 Corbis; 7*br* C. & H. S. Pellant; 8–9 Corbis; 9*tr* G. Brad
Lewis/Science Photo Library; 10–11 (sky) Dynamic Graphic; 10*tr* C. & H. S. Pellant; 10*bl* Corbis; 11 Corbis; 12–13 Geoscience Features;
12*cl* C. & H. S. Pellant; 13*cl* C. & H. S. Pellant; 14–15 Corbis; 15*tl* C. & H. S. Pellant; 15*cr* Science Photo Library; 16*cl* C. & H. S. Pellant;
16–17 Corbis; 17*tl* Geoscience Features; 18–19 Corbis; 19*tl* Frank Lane Picture Library; 19*cr* Frank Lane Picture Library; 20–21 (sky) Dynamic
Graphic; 20–21 (rock) Science Photo Library; 21*tr* Corbis; 21*br* Corbis; 22–23 Corbis; 22*tl* Science Photo Library; 23*tr* Corbis; 24–25 Science
Photo Library; 25*tl* Digital Science; 25*br* Corbis; 26–27 Corbis; 26*bl* Corbis; 27*l* Corbis; 28–29 Corbis; 28*bl* David M. Dennis/Oxford Scientific
Films; 29*tl* Corbis; 30–31 Corbis; 30*b* Science Photo Library; 31*c* Corbis; 32–33 Corbis; 32*bl* Corbis; 33*b* Corbis; 34–35 Corbis; 34*br* Ardea;
35*tl* Science Photo Library; 35*r* Corbis; 36–37 Michael Fogden/Oxford Scientific Films; 37*t* Science Photo Library; 37*cr* Geoscience Features;
38–39 Corbis; 39*tr* Corbis; 39*cl* Science Photo Library; 40–41 David M. Dennis/Oxford Scientific Films; 40*b* Science Photo Library; 41*cr*
Science Photo Library; 42–43 Geoscience Features; 42*bl* Corbis; 43*tr* Corbis; 45*tr* Geoscience Features; 46*tr* Corbis; 48*l* Corbis.

Commissioned photography on pages 44–45 by Geoff Dann; 46–47 by Andy Crawford.
Thank you to models Daniel Newton and Eleanor Davis.

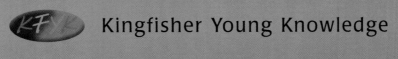

Kingfisher Young Knowledge

Rocks and Fossils

Chris Pellant

Contents

6 What is a rock?

The earth's crust is made of rocks. Some rocks are hard and solid, such as granite. Others are soft, such as sand. All rocks are made of minerals.

Craggy landscape
Here, in the Sierra Nevada mountains, USA, weather has damaged a granite mountain top and broken it into large rounded boulders.

crust – *the earth's outermost layer, some of which lies under oceans*

Grains of granite

Granite is made of different coloured minerals. The pink mineral is called feldspar, the grey one is quartz and the black one is called mica.

minerals – natural substances in the earth's surface that make rocks

8 Rocks from fire

When a volcano erupts, red-hot lava bursts out and gushes downhill as boiling rivers of fire. Slowly the lava cools and hardens into rock. We call this type of rock igneous, which means made from fire.

lava – *molten rock on the earth's surface*

Underground

Igneous rock also forms underground when molten (melted) rock called magma cools down.

Cooling lava

Lava takes a long time to cool. First, a thick skin forms on top, then slowly all the lava turns into solid rock.

magma – molten rock when it is underground

Rough and smooth

As molten rock cools, crystals are formed from the minerals. Large crystals grow if the rock cools slowly. Small crystals grow if the rock cools quickly.

Medium crystals
This microgranite rock has smaller crystals than granite because it cooled more quickly.

Lava columns
Basalt has tiny crystals and can have a smooth surface. It often cools into six-sided columns.

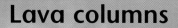

crystals – hard, glassy-looking objects made of minerals

Cracks for climbing

Granite has large crystals. When granite magma cools, cracks form in the rock. Climbers grip the cracks as they climb.

columns – tall, narrow pillars

Second-hand rocks

Sand, mud and pebbles in a river or lake, or on the sea-bed can be turned into rocks called sedimentary rocks. These can be told apart from others because they have layers, or strata.

Shell rock

Limestone is often made of tiny shells. Curved snail-shells can be seen in this rock.

sea-bed – *the bottom of the sea*

sea-cliff

Sandy cliffs
These cliffs in Dorset, UK, are made of layers of compressed sand formed on the sea-bed millions of years ago.

compressed – *tightly pressed together*

Layer by layer

There are three different types of sedimentary rocks. One type is made of the remains of dead sea animals. Another is made of mud, sand or pebbles. The third is made when water evaporates.

Tiny creatures
Limestone is made of the skeletons of millions of tiny sea creatures. It is weathered easily, often forming scenery such as this.

evaporates – when water turns to gas as it dries up

Rock gypsum

Sea-water contains minerals. When it evaporates, minerals stay behind and form rocks such as this gypsum.

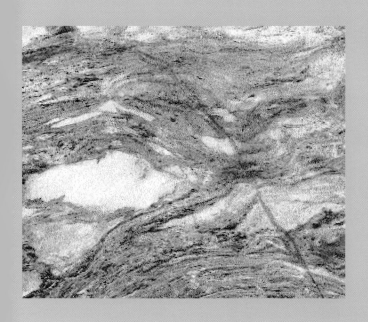

Made of sand

Sandstone is a very common rock. It often forms colourful layers, such as those you can see in this picture.

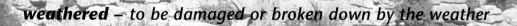

weathered – *to be damaged or broken down by the weather*

Rocks that change

Rocks change when they are heated deep underground – their crystals grow larger. Limestone, a sedimentary rock, turns into a metamorphic rock called marble. Layers in the rock disappear as it takes on a new form.

Fossil layers
Limestone is a rock formed in the sea and contains fossils. These fossils break down when the rock changes into marble.

fossil – any evidence of living things from the past

Smooth marble
Marble has millions of pale crystals made of a mineral called calcite, stuck together tightly like a jigsaw.

Monumental rock
Marble is cut into many different shapes, and used for ornaments, sculptures and gravestones.

metamorphic – a change of form, usually by heat or pressure

Under pressure

As the earth's crust moves, any rocks deep down are twisted and squashed, and their shape is changed by pressure.

Twisted gneiss

Gneiss rock has twisted bands of dark and pale minerals. It used to be granite, and is formed by the greatest pressure.

pressure – when a weight is pressing down on something

Slivers of slate

Slate is made when the pressure underground is not very great. This rock breaks into thin slabs and can be used for roofing.

Silvery schist

Schist is formed in mountainous areas by medium pressure. Its silvery surface is covered with the mineral mica.

mountainous – *an area where there are mountains*

Wear and tear

Rocks do not last for ever. They are battered by the sea on the coasts. High in the mountains, glaciers grind rocks to dust. Rivers carve valleys into the land.

Sandblasted

This arch is all that is left of a huge cliff. Sand carried in the wind blows against it constantly and wears it away.

glaciers – large, slow-moving masses of ice

Deep cuts

Rocks, sand and pebbles carried in rivers pound against the river banks, and can cut deep gorges into the land.

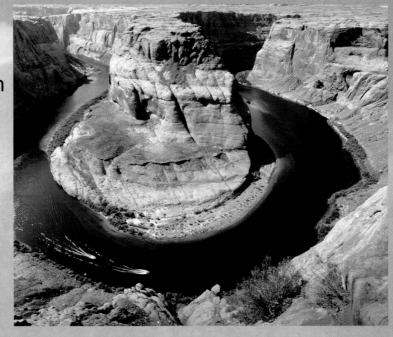

Wave power

Waves hurl rocks and stones at the cliffs, slowly breaking down the coastline.

gorges – deep, steep-sided valleys carved into the land by a river

Rain, roots and ice

Growing roots
Plants grow in cracks in rocks. As their roots grow, they push the cracks further apart.

Rocks are damaged by the weather. They shrink in the cold and expand when it is hot. Rainwater gets into cracks. When the water freezes, the ice expands the cracks and the rock shatters.

expand – get bigger

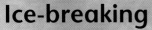

Ice-breaking

This mountain ridge shows how ice can break rocks apart to form jagged points.

Washed away

This rock is a strange shape because rainwater has weathered it over many years.

Rocks from space

There are many rocks in space, of different shapes and sizes. They are called meteorites and are rocks left over from when the planets formed. Sometimes, meteorites crash down to earth.

Impact crater
This huge crater in Arizona, USA, was formed when a gigantic meteorite smashed into earth. It is over a kilometre across – more than the length of 14 jumbo jets.

crater – a hole in the ground made by a meteorite or a volcanic explosion

Explosive rock

When large meteorites hit the ground, they explode. The heat from the explosion melts the rocks around them making glassy stones called tektites.

Hot metal

Most meteorites are made of metal, like this one. As they rush through the sky, they become extremely hot and can be seen as trails of light.

explode – *to blow up, usually with a loud bang*

The uses of rocks

Rocks are used in thousands of ways. Without rocks, there would be no bricks, cement, glass or coal. Most industry is based on the use of rocks.

Potty about clay
Clay is an important rock. As well as being used for pottery, it is used to make cement and even washing powder.

cement – a clay and limestone mixture that is used to make concrete

Angelic rock
Pale marble is a favourite rock for carving into ornaments, such as this angel.

Carved in stone
Many of the world's finest buildings are made from cut rock. Sedimentary rocks can be cut into neat blocks for building, and all rocks can be carved into delicate shapes.

What is a fossil?

Any trace of a plant or animal that lived in the past is a fossil, such as a shell preserved in rock layers for millions of years. The black impressions of delicate ferns and the massive footprints of dinosaurs are also fossils.

Trilobite
This creature lived in the sea hundreds of millions of years ago. Its modern relatives include insects, crabs and spiders.

preserved – *to be kept in good condition over a period of time*

Big bones
These dinosaur bones were uncovered in the Dinosaur National Monument, Colorado, USA.

Uncovering the past
A palaeontologist works very carefully to expose part of a huge dinosaur skeleton at Dinosaur National Monument.

palaeontologist – *someone who studies fossils*

How fossils form

Dead creatures and plants may
be buried in sand or mud. This
is when fossilization begins.
The soft parts of the animal
rot away, while the hard
parts – its shell or bones –
become fossilized.

Stuck fast, forever
This ant is caught in
the sticky resin oozing
from a tree. It will die
there and may
become a fossil.

Fossilized fly

Millions of years ago, this fly
became trapped in resin,
which hardened to amber,
fossilizing the fly.

Ammonites

Ammonites swam in the sea when
dinosaurs roamed the land. They are
close relatives of squids and octopuses.

ammonite

resin – *a very sticky substance that oozes from pine trees*

Ancient sea creatures

Fossils of dead sea creatures lie buried under the constant build-up of muddy and sandy layers on the sea-bed. Trilobites, corals, molluscs and starfish are all common fossils from the ancient seas.

Tropical fossils

Corals build their homes out of limestone, often in tropical seas. Fossil corals tell geologists where these seas were long ago.

molluscs – soft-bodied animals, such as clams and slugs

fossilized fish

Stone starfish
Even delicate animals such as this starfish can be fossilized. This fossil has formed in shale – a sedimentary rock formed on the sea-bed from packed mud.

The age of dinosaurs

Nobody has ever seen a dinosaur because they became extinct millions of years ago. We only know about dinosaurs from finding fossils of their bones, footprints and eggs.

dinosaur fossil footprint

Buried in rock

This Stegosaurus fossil was found buried in Wyoming, in the USA. It clearly shows the shape of the dinosaur.

extinct – when all animals or plants of a certain type die, and none are left

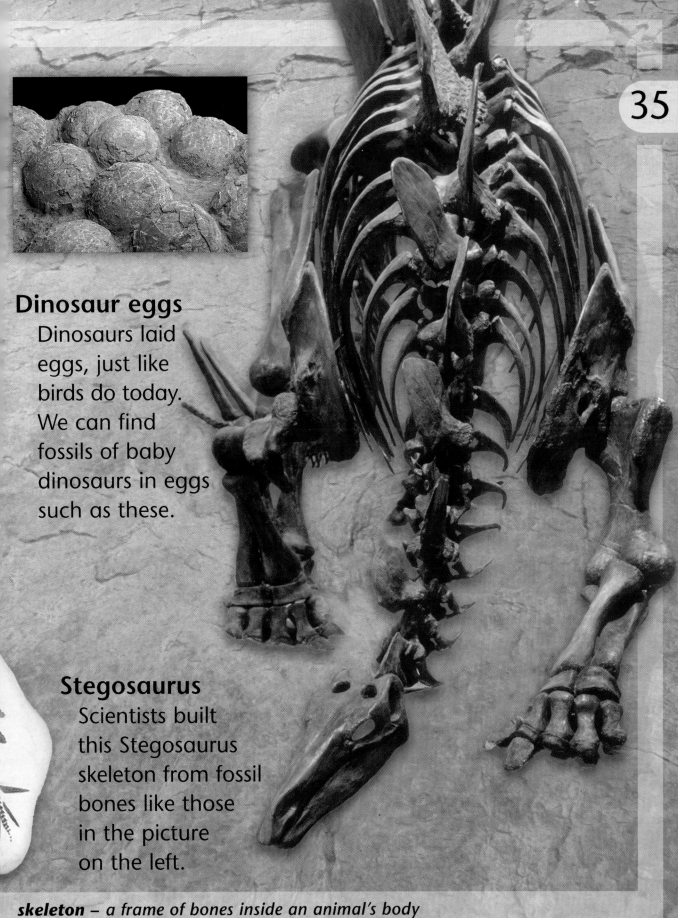

Dinosaur eggs

Dinosaurs laid eggs, just like birds do today. We can find fossils of baby dinosaurs in eggs such as these.

Stegosaurus

Scientists built this Stegosaurus skeleton from fossil bones like those in the picture on the left.

skeleton – *a frame of bones inside an animal's body*

Fossil plants

Fossils of stems and tree trunks are common, especially in rocks that contain seams of coal. Among the seams, even fossils of delicate ferns may be found.

Stone trees

These trees were changed by fossilization – they are now made of a mineral called silica, instead of wood.

seams – thin layers of a substance, such as coal

From old...

Delicate, beautiful fern leaves are fossilized as thin layers of carbon between the layers of rock.

...to modern

A modern fern is just like fossil ferns hundreds of millions of years old.

carbon – a solid, black substance of which coal is made

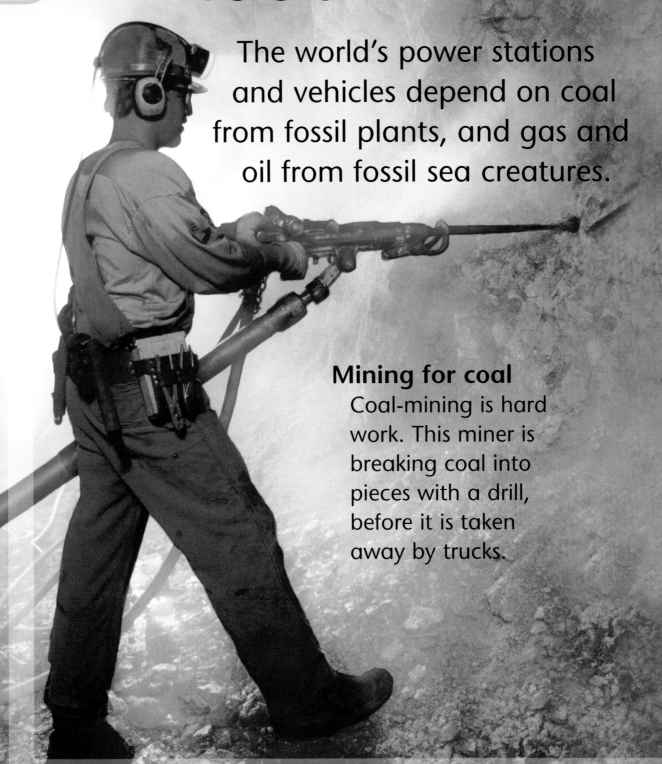

Fossil fuels

The world's power stations and vehicles depend on coal from fossil plants, and gas and oil from fossil sea creatures.

Mining for coal

Coal-mining is hard work. This miner is breaking coal into pieces with a drill, before it is taken away by trucks.

fuels – substances used for producing heat or power by burning

Fossils for driving

Oil is a fossil fuel from which many products, including petrol and diesel oil, are made.

Poisonous fuel

Coal is a black shiny rock. It has been used as a fuel for hundreds of years. However, when it is burned, poisonous smoke billows out and causes much pollution.

pollution – chemicals, gases and other materials that damage the environment

Clues from fossils

Fossils tell us about life millions of years ago. Scientists can reconstruct bodies of extinct creatures and study how animals and plants have evolved.

Alive and well

The coelacanth fish was known only as a fossil. Then, in 1938, living coelacanths were caught off the South African coast.

reconstruct – *to rebuild and show how something looked*

Historic footsteps
These footprints, made in soft mud over three million years ago, show that our ancestors walked upright at that time.

archaeopteryx

Archaeopteryx
This is one of the most famous fossils. The skeleton resembles a small dinosaur, but there are impressions of feathers. Experts believe that modern birds are descended from dinosaurs.

evolved – to have changed gradually over time

How to find fossils

Fossils can be found near cliffs or quarries, or in other areas that have sedimentary rock. However, these can be dangerous places, and you must never visit them without an adult.

Cliff-hanger
Palaeontologists go to many different places to search for fossils and it can be dangerous work. This fossil-hunter is carefully unearthing fossils on a steep slope.

quarries – places from which stone is cut, usually for use in building

Beach treasure

Fossils may fall
from cliffs and
land on the
beaches below.
Be careful around
cliffs and beware
of falling rocks.

Warning!

When rock is quarried, fossils
are often unearthed. Never
go to working quarries
though – they can be
very dangerous.

44 Fun with fossils

You will need
- 5 balls of coloured dough
- Shells

Roll the dough into flat cakes. Sprinkle the first cake with shells. These will be your fossils.

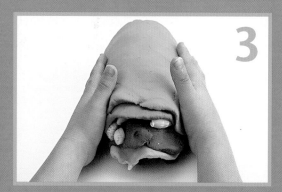

Push the sides together to make an arch. This happens when rocks are squeezed together.

Making mountains
Layers of rock can be squashed together and forced up to make mountains. Any fossils in the layers then come to the surface.

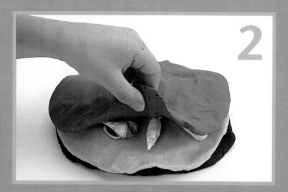

Add two more layers of dough and shells. Then put two layers of dough on top. Do not put any shells in the top two layers.

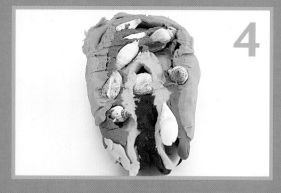

Ask an adult to slice off the top. The first layers put down are now in the middle. They are the oldest layers and have the oldest fossils.

Amazing ammonites

Make your own fossil with modelling clay and moulding plaster. Use a real fossil or a shell to make a cast.

You will need
- Modelling clay
- Fossil or shell
- Moulding plaster
- Cup and spoon
- Paint
- Paintbrush

Roll some modelling clay into a ball. Press your fossil or shell, patterned side down, into the clay to make the cast.

Mix some moulding plaster with water in a cup and carefully spoon or pour it into the cast. Leave to set.

Once your fossil has set hard, carefully lift it from the cast. You may be able to use the cast again to make more fossils.

Your fossil is now ready to paint. Use any colours you like. Copy the colours of the shell or fossil, or paint it in brighter colours.

46 Rocks around you

Rock collection

When you start rock collecting, label your rocks and record where you found them to organize your collection.

An eggbox is an ideal place for your collection. Use a different box for different types or colours of rock. Paint your eggbox.

You will need

- Eggbox
- Paint
- Paintbrush
- Cup for holding water
- Magnifying glass
- Sticky labels
- Notepad
- Pen

Examine the rock using a magnifying glass. You may be able to see the different coloured minerals that form the rock.

Number all your rocks, starting from 1. Write the number of the rock on a sticky label and stick it onto the rock.

In your notepad, write the number, where and when you found the rock, and the rock type. If you do not know the type, leave a space to fill it in later.

Finally, once the paint on your eggbox has dried, put your rock into it making sure the label can be seen. Congratulations! You have begun your rock collection.

How are rocks used?

Rocks are used in many ways. Look around you at home and outside, and draw the rocks that you see.

You will need
- Notepad
- Pen

You may see rocks as part of a wall, pavement or building. How many different uses of rocks can you find?

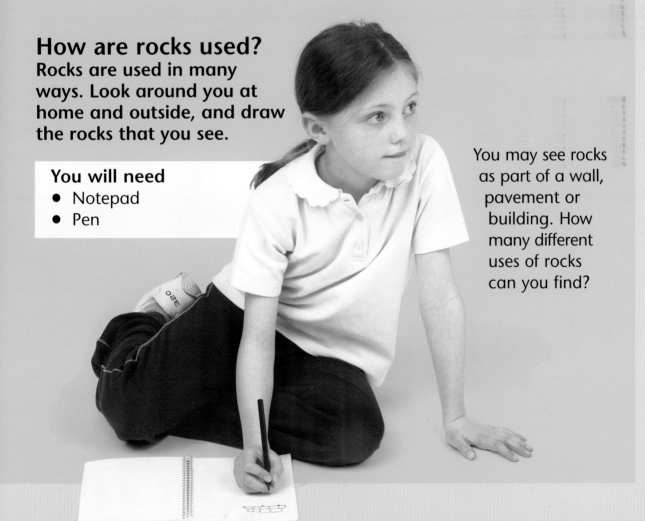

Index